CHRISTMAS
BELLS & BLESSINGS

Hazel Jaycox Brown

Abingdon Press

Table of Contents

HANGING OF THE GREENS 5
—2 or more readers, plus special music and helpers to decorate.

   Time: 15 minutes for reading written script + activity + music +
   prayer. Can be done in a half hour or stretched into an hour.
   Synopsis: The Gospel is presented, giving every type of decoration a
   spiritual significance and some enlightenment on tradition.

ADVENT 11
*—Something for each of the four Sundays of Advent. Youth or
adults can present these, using two or more people.*

   Time: Eight to ten minutes for each, including music and prayer.
   Synopsis: Two Advents are discussed: Jesus' first coming and our
preparation for His second coming. Woven into these discussions are:
Sin's awfulness, the Plan prepared, a people prepared, the Law given,
and prophecies fulfilled. Many of God's people were unprepared for
the first Advent. Are we ready for the second one?

ANGEL TALK 23
—a play for 11-21 adults, youth, or juniors.

   Time: 10 minutes for script plus music.
   Synopsis: It's about time for the big announcement on earth.
Rehearsal for this has been called, but angels are so busy looking
after their charges on earth, it's almost impossible to get them
together for practice. The world badly needs a Savior.

BIRTHDAY REFLECTION 29
—2 women, 1 man, and narrator.

   Time: 13 minutes.
Synopsis: Mary, Joseph, and two-year-old Jesus have just arrived back
home in Nazareth, coming from Egypt. They stop at Mary's widowed
mother's house for the night. She has heard very little about the
events of the past two years and wants to know. This emotional drama
reenacts what might have taken place at such an event.

CHRISTMAS BELLS AND BLESSINGS 37

—*A contemporary play for 13 to 29 children. Adults could play adult parts, including a female or male senior citizen.*

Time: 20 minutes as written here. Suggestions are included to make it longer if desired.

Synopsis: The children have just finished their Christmas play. They gather to sympathize with Jerry because his dear great-grandmother had broken her hip and is in the hospital. This was the first Christmas program she had missed at church in 86 years. They decide to go to the hospital the next day to present the program to her in person. Of course, all are rewarded in this emotional drama. Several lessons are learned—true caring and giving, the Christmas story with its significance, and something that's better than a good Christmas celebration here on earth.

PORTRAITS OF MARY 51

—*First person drama. Narrator needed.*

Time: 22 minutes for the written script.

Synopsis: With great emotion Mary tells about Gabriel's appearance to her, about Joseph, about the events surrounding Jesus' birth, about Jesus' growing up, about witnessing his death and afterward. The Gospel is clearly presented from a mother's vantage point—Mary's.

HANGING OF THE GREENS

TO THE LEADER—*Assign parts to two as portrayed in this script or several. Pre-assigned "decorators" (any age who can handle them) can come from the audience to place decorations as readers ask for them during the program. They should know ahead how and where to place their item.*

If you have a tree in your sanctuary, string the lights on it prior to this service. A moment is inserted in the script for children and young people to come from the audience to place things. First will be the greens, the second lights, the third sounds. Let's start with singing together.

POSSIBLE SONGS— *"We Gather Together"* and *"Come, Thou Long-Expected Jesus"*

PRAYER

(Begin background music—organ or tape.)

READER 1: We'll begin with the placing of the wreaths. *(Wait until placed.)* A wreath is symbolic of a crown. Long ago, crowns were given for prizes. They were usually made of leaves and were bestowed to give honor and glory. In placing these wreaths let us give honor and glory to Jesus, who came into the world to be our Savior. He alone is worthy, for He brought us victory over sin and death.

Reader 2: We should also remember the *crown* of thorns He wore, while suffering for our sins. Hebrews 2:9 says: "But we see Jesus, who was made a little lower than the angels, now crowned with glory and honor because he suffered death, so that by the grace of God he might taste death for everyone." Let's crown Him King of our lives.

Reader 1: Please place the greens in each window. *(Wait until finished.)* Now place the greens on the altar. *(Wait.)* Now other greens. *(Wait until all are in place. Do not yet light any candles or lights placed with the greens.)* Thank you.
Evergreens, including holly, are most commonly used at Christmas. Some variety of holly grows in almost every

5

country. In former times the holly tree was called the holy tree and was commonly displayed in churches.

READER 2: The thorny leaves of holly remind us of the crown of thorns worn by Jesus when crucified. The red berries represent drops of blood—His blood shed to atone for our sins. Remember the significance of holly greens at Christmas, then praise and thank the Lord for what He has done for us.

SONG— *"Crown Him with Many Crowns" (verses 1, 3, 5)*

READER 1: The enduring evergreen tree with its branches is appropriate for Christmas. Jesus died on a tree to save us from our sins. This is an enduring provision. Though we seek to make our Christmas trees beautiful, nothing compares to the beauty of what resulted from His death on that cross. God, in tremendous love, gave His only begotten Son to save the world. Because Jesus loved us, He willingly left heaven to suffer and die for you and me. He became the Sacrificial Lamb. What matchless, wondrous beauty is this! Our greatest endeavors to create Christmas beauty are ashes in comparison.

READER 2: Pine cones are more than ornaments to the evergreen tree. Within them new seed is produced. As the wind blows, the cone faithfully scatters seed to provide new life. This is symbolic of what you and I are to become. After the seed of Christ is implanted in us, the Holy Spirit instructs and prepares us for gospel seed sowing. If we are faithful, others will experience new birth from our seed.

READER 1: Green reminds us of growth. Are we ever green, ever growing? Is the Holy Spirit in control of our lives? How do we handle the tough parts of life? We all have them. These should help us scatter the seed of God's love effectively. God is the God of hard times as well as the good. With the Holy Spirit in control, our growth in His Word will flourish and we will effectively spread His seed. Then the gospel will be reproduced.

READER 2: John 1:1-3 says: "In the beginning [before creation] was the Word [Jesus], and the Word was with God, and the Word was God. He was with God in the beginning. Through him all things were made; without him nothing was made that has been made." After creation, humankind sinned. A way must be provided to blot out our sin. A plan was made; Jesus would become human flesh and live here on earth. Through example and word, He would teach us.

SPECIAL SONG— *"Ivory Palaces"*

READER 1: Because "without the shedding of blood there is no forgiveness" of sin (Hebrews 9:22), Jesus suffered and shed His blood for my sin and yours. Blameless, He became the Supreme sacrifice for our sins. That price paid enables us to have *everlasting* life.

READER 2: Jesus said in John 3:14-16: " . . . so the Son of Man (Jesus) must be lifted up, that everyone who believes in him may have eternal life. For God so loved the world that he gave his one and only Son, that whoever believes in him shall not perish, but have *eternal [everlasting] life.*"

READER 1: Notice the word—*eternal*. That means without end, everlasting, infinity. Ever-green, signifies no death, ever-lastingness. Christ came to bring *everlasting life*. That's our inheritance as children of God. During this season, let evergreens remind you of the *everlastingness of God* Himself, and the loving provision for *our everlastingness.*

SONG— *"Hallelujah! What A Savior"*

(LIGHTS OUT— *READERS USE FLASHLIGHT, AND ORGANIST USES SMALL LIGHT)*

READER 2: Jesus said, " . . . I am the Light of the World," in John 9:5. In 12:46, He further states, "I have come into the world as a light, so that no one who believes in me should stay in darkness." The apostle Paul in Ephesians 5 explains more,

"For you were once in darkness, but now you are light in the Lord. Live as children of light . . . and find out what pleases the Lord. Have nothing to do with the fruitless deeds of darkness, but rather expose them." *(Verses 8, 10, 11).*

READER 1: Without light there is darkness. Jesus came and His light shone forth to the world. But there's more. Please light our windows. *(Wait.)* Notice the room is a bit brighter. Is anyone besides us benefiting from these lights? Maybe someone outside is cheered by the sight. Maybe someone outside can find his way by coming to the light. Please light the altar candles. *(Wait.)* It's better, but still dim. Now please light the rest of the candles placed around. *(Wait.)* It keeps getting brighter. *But what if a few people scattered in our audience here lit and held a candle? That would create more light, wouldn't it? Then if each one holding a lighted candle would light their neighbor's candle, twice as much light would radiate. If everyone in our sanctuary held a light, we would be a torch—a lighthouse.

(*The reader can just read this last part. If it is actually done as read, however, the result is dramatic. A 6-inch candle works nicely. Cover a 4-inch square cardboard with aluminum foil. Cut a + in the center. Insert candle through the cut to protect hands from hot wax. Small children can share with an adult. Practice safety. This might also be done with small flashlights.)

READER 2: *(If you did the * above, say,* "Extinguish your candle carefully. After the wax has hardened, hand them down to the end of the pew or put aside." *You choose how best to lay them aside.)*

Jesus is the light of Christmas. As we accept that Light, Jesus, into our lives and share it, our world becomes brighter. Do you see the beauty of this wonderful plan? God loved us; Jesus brought the light of God to earth. We, as receivers of this love and light, will naturally share with others. Our light makes a difference in our world. Without it, we live in darkness.

READER 1: For many years lights have been a part of Christmas.

Martin Luther is credited with decorating the first tree. While walking through a forest one Christmas Eve, he noticed the stars shining through the evergreen trees. Greatly impressed by that picture, he chopped down a tree and brought it home to his family. He attempted to share what he had seen by decorating it with lighted candles. Now, may we please have our Christmas lights. *(Christmas tree and/or other special lights. Wait a few moments; then add the following if appropriate.)* We shall add more decorations. *(Balls and anything else to go on the tree.)*

READER 2: When observing the evergreen this Christmas, remember an everlasting Father made everlasting life available to you and me. As I accept it, I am a recipient of Jesus' light. I must share this light with others around me. We want to pass it on.

SONG— *"Pass It On"*

READER 1: Many other symbols and sounds are represented at Christmas. Some of them come directly from the Christmas story—gift giving, the star, the angels, the stable scene with Mary, Joseph, the Baby, the manger, the shepherds, the Magi [wisemen].

The poinsettia, growing wild in Mexico, was brought to this country and has become a Christmas symbol. The shape of the red "flower" is like a many-pointed star, symbolizing the star of Bethlehem, and the red for the shed blood at Calvary.

READER 2: The two primary sounds of Christmas are bells and carols. For many centuries, bells were used to give messages. Their vibrations reach far, and catch the attention of those in sound's way. They can call people together, or they can send good news. For both reasons Christmas bells peal to celebrate the birth of Christ our Savior, the greatest of good news for all the world. Listen now to the bells.

SPECIAL MUSIC—*by a handbell choir, bells ringing, synthesizer, tape or whatever playing "Joy to the World."*

READER 1: People have sung carols at festivals and church services celebrating Christmas for many centuries now. Singing them reminds us again of the precious old, old story. Caroling spreads the Good News. We are blessed and filled with joy as we sing them, and those listening are also.

READER 2: Christ's coming brought new *hope* to a crumbling world. We as His children have the promise of everlasting life—the *Ultimate Hope.* His coming demonstrated *love* in abundance. Never had the world understood the extent of *God's love* until Jesus came, dying for our sins—*Amazing Love.* His coming brought *joy* to hearts surrendered to Christ. He relieves us from the burdens of sin and the cares of life, and replaces them with abundant life—*Joy Unspeakable.* His coming brought *peace* to those accepting Jesus as Savior. This concept was foreign to the world until the Prince of Peace came in Person—*Perfect Peace.*

READER 1: Do you possess that Ultimate Hope, that Amazing Love, that Joy Unspeakable, and that Perfect Peace now? It's available to you. Accept the Supreme Gift, if you haven't, this Christmas—today. Live for Him and claim these gifts as yours, now. Come, by faith. Repent. Believe His promise to receive you.

READER 2: As we live for Him this Christmas, let us remember the pine cone. Let us be sowers of His seed, ever growing, ever glowing with His light. Let us share the Good News to those without hope, without love, without joy, without peace. Let's join together in pealing out the Good News . . . JESUS CHRIST IS BORN.

SONG—*"Ring the Bells"* or *"I Heard the Bells on Christmas Day"*

CLOSING PRAYER—Pastor

FIRST SUNDAY OF ADVENT

MUSIC BACKGROUND— *"Come, Thou Long-Expected Jesus"*
or *"Thou Didst Leave Thy Throne"*

READER 1: Even though the word *ADVENT* does not appear in the
Bible, its meaning is there—the coming of Christ. The
dictionary says Advent can focus on either Christ's first
coming or His second. We will consider both.
Actually, a person must first experience a personal Advent
of Christ's rebirth within, in order to anticipate the second
one. Then the true Christian will feel the wonder and joy
of Christ's first coming. As a child of God learns to daily
trust, obey, and live for the Lord, that child will look
forward to the Second Advent.

READER 2: God—the Father, the Son and the Holy Spirit—saw the
world's need for a Savior in Adam's time. Satan, coming in
the form of a snake, tempted Eve. She listened, then
yielded. Adam joined her in disobedience to God. They
sinned.

In Genesis 3:15 God spoke to the snake, and said, " And I
will put enmity between you and the woman, and between
your offspring and hers; he will crush your head and you
will strike his heel." The offspring of woman was Christ.
His death on the cross won the victory over sin and death.
God's people look forward to eternity with Christ, where
all pain, tears, and death have been removed.

READER 1: God loved us so much. Sin was destructive; it separated
God and humanity. A way for salvation was needed. To
fulfill the prophecy in Genesis 3, God planned for a
"chosen" people. A righteous man called Abraham was
chosen to be the patriarch of this nation. God would
reveal Himself in special ways to the descendants of
Abraham and Jacob.

The written Law was prepared and given to this people
through Moses, so they'd know right from wrong. They

better understood how awful sin is in God's sight. Redemption was necessary, a shedding of blood. So God's people, the Jews, were carefully instructed in the offering of sacrifices for atonement. They were to be examples of godliness to the rest of the world. Even though many failed in this, some righteous people faithfully spoke God's message.

God had further plans. Prophets told of a coming Messiah. He would save people from their sins by becoming the ultimate sacrifice. Jesus would be the King of Kings and Lord of Lords.

CONGREGATION: *(Read together.)* Philippians 2:5-11. *(Include this in your bulletin or make an insert.)*

READER 2: During Jesus' ministry, many people thought He was the Messiah. But when He was brought to trial, then mocked, beaten and crucified instead of becoming king, they turned their backs. They failed to understand the prophecies of old—that Jesus come twice, first as a Suffering Servant—Redeemer. Later, He would come as Lord and King. Their sins and selfish desires blinded them from seeing Truth.

READER 1: We might look back and judge those people harshly. Could they not see Jesus doing all kinds of miraculous things? But they failed to see. Their ignorance of God's Word, their indifference and their sin blinded them. In spite of all the preparations made by God, most people missed His first coming.

READER 2: Today we have greater perspective and enlightenment. We know Jesus will come again. But do we live like it? Are we daily reading God's Word, so we can obey, overcome evil, and be ready? Are we waiting and watching with anticipation? Are we concerned about others in spiritual darkness? Are we preparing for Christ's coming today?

BRIEF PRAYER—*(An extemporaneous one or this optional one.)*

We praise You, O Lord, that You loved us so much that You made provision for forgiveness of sins. Thank you, Jesus, for coming and being faithful unto death, so we could have victory. Examine our hearts here today. May each of us be fully ready for that glorious Second Advent. Help us to be faithful in all things, and to witness to others of Your saving power. In Jesus' precious name, we pray, Amen.

CANDLE LIGHTING— _____ *will light the first candle of preparation.*

SONG—*(Congregational or Special) Here are some possibilities:*
   "Redeeming Love"
   "Jesus Is Coming Again"
   "Soon and Very Soon"

SECOND SUNDAY OF ADVENT

RELIGHT last week's candle *before the service begins.*

BACKGROUND MUSIC— *"O Come, All Ye Faithful"*

READER 1: Last week we were again made aware of humanity's sin, God's love, and His plan. The world could learn about God's law and provision for redemption through His chosen people. Sin is so terrible that the shedding of blood was the price for forgiveness. Animal sacrifices came first, but were inadequate. The Supreme Sacrifice must be made. The Messiah, God's only begotten Son, became the Sacrificial Lamb.

READER 2: Nearly every book in the Old Testament made reference to the coming Messiah. But people were too preoccupied to pay much attention. However, God had plans: "For God so loved the world that he gave his one and only Son, that whoever believes in him shall not perish but have eternal life. For God did not send his Son into the world to condemn the world, but to save the world through him." *(John 3:16, 17.)*

READER 1: The stage was made ready for Advent One. Over three hundred years before the birth of Jesus, Alexander the Great had conquered much of the known world. He then made Greek the universal language, so everyone had to learn it. The way was thus prepared for spreading the gospel through a common language. Roman rule meant a peace of sorts existed throughout the known world. It also allowed people to travel across boundaries without difficulty. Yes, this was a unique time in history.

READER 2: But more preparation was necessary. Someone had to introduce the Messiah. A witness would help provide credibility and proof of whom Jesus was.

Zechariah, a priest, and his wife Elizabeth lived upright lives in the sight of God. They obeyed the Law and regulations. This childless couple was too old for childbearing. But with God all things are possible.

READER 1: Zechariah was much like us. He prayed and prayed for a favor from God, but was shocked when it came. Zechariah had long prayed for a son. One day Gabriel, an angel of the Lord, told him his prayer was answered. Zechariah could hardly believe it. As a result, he was left speechless until after John was born and named.

READER 2: But God told Zechariah at that appearance something about their special son. His name would be John, and he would be great in the sight of the Lord. John was never to taste strong drink. He would be filled with the Holy Spirit, even from birth. John would bring many Israelites back to the Lord their God in the spirit and power of Elijah. His job was to prepare the people for the coming of the Lord.

READER 1: In the sixth month after conception, Elizabeth had a visitor. Mary, who had also been recently visited by Gabriel, came. Upon her arrival, Elizabeth's baby recognized the presence of the Holy One of Israel and leaped within Elizabeth's womb.

READER 2: You know the rest of the story. As an adult John the Baptist preached the gospel of repentance before Jesus began His public ministry. John baptized Jesus and introduced Him to his hearers as the Messiah. He knew Jesus' ministry would overshadow his, because he told his hearers, "He must become greater; I must become less." *(John 3:30)*

READER 1: John the Baptist was a key player in preparation for Jesus' ministry. Malachi 3:1 tells us this prophecy concerning John: "See, I will send my messenger, who will prepare the way before me. Then suddenly the Lord you are seeking will come to his temple; the messenger of the covenant, whom you desire, will come," says the Lord Almighty.

READER 1: God saw to it that every word of prophecy for the first Advent came true. Yet so many were unprepared, unaccepting, because they were blinded by ignorance and sinful living. God is making sure that every word of prophecy leading up to His Advent will be fulfilled. Much of it already has. The stage seems nearly ready. It can happen any day. Are you prepared? Are you watching in anticipation?

BRIEF PRAYER—*(Extemporaneous or this optional one)*

We praise Your Name that You did not leave us in ignorance, O Lord. We have Your Word to read and to know how to live a life pleasing to You. Help us to believe Your Word and to live accordingly. Help us to be ready and watching in anticipation. Help us to increase awareness in others that You are coming soon, and that You are the only Hope we have. Praise Your wonderful Name. Amen.

CANDLE LIGHTING— _____ *will light the second candle of preparation.*

SONG—*Congregational or special possibilities:*
"The Savior Is Waiting"
"What If It Were Today?"
"Is It the Crowning Day?" or any from last week's list.

THIRD SUNDAY OF ADVENT

RELIGHT the last two week's candles *before the service begins.*

BACKGROUND MUSIC— *"Take My Life and Let It Be"*

READER 1: Even though God had told His people over and over about the coming Messiah, most were not ready when He came. They failed to recognize Him.

READER 2: But some people sincerely awaited with hearts prepared for the Messiah's coming. Two such people were Mary and Joseph of Nazareth. Both were descendants of David, the line through which prophecy had said the Messiah would come. They were betrothed. This pledge for marriage was as binding as marriage itself. At this point they were yet living apart.

READER 1: One day Mary met an angel named Gabriel. Let's read about their time together from Luke 1:26-38. You can find it _____ *(In bulletin, an insert or handout. Read responsively or together; instruct the congregation.)*

READER 2: We know such a request from God must have brought major concerns to Mary's mind. She was yet unmarried. The law allowed death by stoning for any woman found in such a plight. At least her good reputation would suffer. Would anyone believe the true story, if she told it? Most of all, would Joseph? He would be within his rights to back out of his commitment to her. She must have thought of these things before answering Gabriel.

READER 1: But Mary loved God with her whole heart, and committed herself in obedience, no matter what might happen. Often blind obedience is necessary to receive God's greatest blessings. This is exercising faith. God had made a huge request of this one whose heart was prepared for the Messiah's coming. She willingly accepted it.

Elizabeth later saw her and declared, " . . . Blessed are you

17

among women. . . . why am I so favored, that the mother of my Lord should come to me?" *(Luke 1:42, 43)*. That recognition was a gift to Mary.

READER 2: But what should Joseph do? Did he really want her with someone else's child? The Scripture says he was a righteous man and did not want to expose her to public disgrace, [so] he had in mind to divorce her quietly. *(Matthew 1:19)* This seemed reasonable at first.

READER 1: Then God sent Joseph an angel who assured him, " . . . do not be afraid to take Mary home as your wife, because what is conceived in her is from the Holy Spirit." *(Matthew 1:20)* I believe Joseph would have obeyed with just that much knowledge, for he too had a heart prepared for the Messiah's coming.

READER 2: But the angel told him more. "She will give birth to a son, and you are to give him the name Jesus, because he will save his people from their sins." Then Matthew says: All of this took place to fulfill what the Lord said through the prophet: "The virgin will be with child and will give birth to a son, and they will call him Immanuel'—which means 'God with us.' " *(Verses 21-23)*. This would be the fulfillment of prophecy.

READER 1: Joseph had a heart to obey, to please God. So he took Mary home with him as is wife. Joseph and Mary were examples to us as precious servants of the Lord—willing to do whatever He asked. All of this preparation was for Advent One.

READER 2: Are you the Lord's servant today? Is your dedication to the Lord enough that God can trust you to do a special work for Him? Are you willing to do what God asks in preparation for Advent Two?

BRIEF PRAYER—*(Extemporaneous or this optional prayer)*

We praise and thank You for coming to earth so long ago.

We praise You for the examples of Mary and Joseph, for their willingness to do what You asked them to do. Forgive us for flimsy dedication, puny consecration, and selfish ways. Help each of us to say here today, "Yes, Lord." May our hearts and the hearts of those around us be truly prepared for Advent Two. In the precious name of Jesus we pray. Amen.

CANDLE LIGHTING— _____ *will light the third candle of preparation.*

SONG—*(Here are some possibilities for a congregational or special song:)*
"Take My Life and Let It Be"
"I'll Live For Him"
"O Come, O Come, Emmanuel"

FOURTH SUNDAY OF ADVENT

RELIGHT the last three week's candles *before the service begins.*

BACKGROUND MUSIC— *"Even So, Lord Jesus, Come"*

READER 1: For that first Advent, God prepared the hearts of those turned in to Him. Simeon and Anna were two more examples. Before Jesus' birth, it had been revealed to them that they would not die before seeing the promised Messiah. They, though elderly, anticipated His coming. One day Simeon, moved by the Holy Spirit, went into the temple courts in Jerusalem. There he saw and recognized the Baby instantly. Mary and Joseph were amazed. Later, Anna also saw and recognized Him as Messiah. She responded with thanksgiving and began witnessing to others.

READER 2: Others beside Jews were waiting for the Messiah also. God had prepared the hearts of some Gentiles too.

Many Jews had been scattered throughout the empires of prevailing conquerors after captivity. Some of these devout Jews, including Daniel, had shared God's Word and prophecies with non-Jews. Some Gentiles had embraced Judaism fully. These converts were called proselytes.

READER 1: Others believed the message of the known Scriptures, but did not become Jews. An example was the Zoroastrians *(zoe roh ASS tree uns).* The Magi or wisemen came from a such a group. They were Gentiles from the East looking for the King of the Jews in Jerusalem. An extraordinary star had caught their interest and led them to this point.

READER 2: Let's read together the account from Matthew 2:1-11. Please find it in _____ . *(Bulletin or insert)*

READER 1: Prophecy was fulfilled over and over. Matthew 2:6 was a quotation from Micah 5:2 in the Old Testament. Matthew 2 has another Old Testament quotation. Verses 14 and 15 say: So he [Joseph] got up, took the child and his mother during the night and left for Egypt, where he stayed until the death of Herod. *And so was fulfilled what the Lord had said through the prophet: "Out of Egypt I called my son."* Those words came from Hosea 11:1.

READER 2: Another quotation in Matthew 2:16-18 reads: "When Herod realized that he had been outwitted by the Magi, he was furious, and he gave orders to kill all the boys in Bethlehem and its vicinity who were two years old and under, in accordance with the time he had learned from the Magi. *Then what was said through the prophet Jeremiah [31:15] was fulfilled: 'A voice is heard in Ramah, weeping and great mourning, Rachel weeping for her children and refusing to be comforted because they are no more.'"*

READER 1: The Magi were key players in the fulfillment of Jewish prophecy concerning the Messiah. These Gentiles were a prepared group. Their knowledge and unwavering faith surely must have astonished Joseph and Mary as their gifts.

READER 2: One of the best proofs of the Bible's validity and authority is prophecy fulfilled. Over and over in the Old Testament, God had people through whom He sent forth His Word. Included in those words was much prophecy. Kingdoms would rise and fall, but not without much forewarning by God's prophets. God's Word is true. Every jot and tittle of prophecy will be fulfilled. Most of it has been already. We are assured that JESUS IS COMING SOON—again. ARE YOU PREPARED FOR ADVENT TWO? Are you helping others to be ready? How will this reminder change your Christmas this year?

BRIEF PRAYER—*(Extemporaneous or this one)*

We praise You, O Lord, for the availability, the validity and the faithfulness of Your Word. It not only tells us about what is yet to come, but it provides signs and how we can be ready. We bow before you here today—to worship, to see better who You are and make right our relationship with You. We bring You the gift of ourselves, and place it at your feet here this morning. Help us to truly celebrate Advent One in the light and spirit of Advent Two. We pray in the power of Jesus' name. Amen.

CANDLE LIGHTING: _____ will light the fourth candle of preparation.

SONG—*Congregational or special. Here are suggestions:*
Any mentioned before in this series.
"He's still the King of Kings"
"What A Day That Will Be"

ANGEL TALK

PLACE—Heaven

TIME—The day Christ is to be born.

SCENE—*Angels are everywhere—most moving gracefully around. Visiting within small groups takes place, while being alert to the main action. Some may hum or whistle a praise tune. Some watch below, shaking their heads in disbelief at what they are seeing. Over in a corner is a screen with chairs behind it. A sign on the screen says, "This Way to Earth." Angels disappear behind the screen when it's their time to make a rescue on earth, as stated in the script.*

CHARACTERS—*21 or less if parts are combined. For adults, teens, and/or children. Those playing parts should feel the message. They should respond to what's going on appropriately and spontaneously throughout the entire skit.*

CAST—

NARRATOR	
GABRIEL	
ANGEL ORGANIZER	
ANGEL #3	ANGEL #12
ANGEL #4	ANGEL #13
ANGEL #5	ANGEL #14
ANGEL #6	ANGEL #15
ANGEL #7	ANGEL #16
ANGEL #8	ANGEL #17
ANGEL #9	ANGEL #18
ANGEL #10	ANGEL #19
ANGEL #11	ANGEL #20

COSTUMES—*Can be as simple as everyone wearing a white top with dark trousers or skirt, plus a halo. Make halos by tying the ends of an 18 to 24-inch gold or silver Christmas garland together. These lie nicely on the head. Make the costumes as elaborate or simple as you wish.*

NARRATOR: The Bible says in Psalm 91:9-12 "If you make the Most High your dwelling . . . then no harm will befall you, . . . For he will command his angels concerning you to guard you in all your ways; they will lift you up in their hands. . . ." (The *King James Version* says, " . . . he shall give his angels charge over thee. . . . ")

Folks, this is heaven (*pointing to the platform*). The angels are extremely busy going to and from the earth taking care of their charges. But wait! This is THE BIG, BIG DAY in all of time and eternity.

ANGEL ORGANIZER: *(Claps hands vigorously together trying to get everyone's attention.)* Everyone! Please listen! *(All stop to listen, but some keep watching below.)* God has just given the word. TONIGHT is the night—the BIG, BIG NIGHT.

ANGEL #5: What's so big about tonight?

ANGEL #10: Yeah, what's so special tonight?

ANGEL #9: I'm needed below. Gotta go in a hurry. *(He leaves.)*

ANGEL ORGANIZER: Do you remember nine months ago when Gabriel was sent on a special mission down to earth?

ANGEL #17: How can we forget? Heaven hasn't been the same without Jesus here.

ANGEL #6: Oh, yes! Gabriel was sent down to a young maiden. Now what was her name?

ANGEL #4: Excuse me, I'm needed below in a hurry! *(She exits.)*

ANGEL #11: Mary. You remember the Jewish young girl who was engaged to Joseph.

(Angel #9 returns, shaking his head.)

ANGEL #8: Emergency below. I'll be back as soon as possible. *(Leaves.)*

ANGEL ORGANIZER: I must go too. Please stick around. We have to rehearse for tonight. *(Leaves.)*

ANGEL #17: I have to run too. My charge seems to need me every time I turn around. *(Leaves.)*

GABRIEL: Mary was one frightened little girl when I appeared to her. I reassured her that the Lord was *very, very* pleased with her. I told her she would be blessed above other women. She was puzzled.

ANGEL #20: I doubt if Mary was aware that you, Gabriel, were her angel—the one in charge of her. She failed to understand fully that God was sending you to her on a *very special* mission. God rarely makes his angel work visible to people.

GABRIEL: I explained that God had chosen her to bear His Son. That she would carry Him the full nine months in her womb. Mary was more puzzled than ever. She asked, "How can this be?"

ANGEL #9: I'll sure be glad when Jesus is born, maybe our work will get easier—GOTTA GO. *(Leaves.)*

(Angel Organizer and Angel #17 bump into Angel #9 as he leaves.)

ANGEL #11: My turn to go too. *(Leaves.)*

ANGEL ORGANIZER: Now can we practice, or are we still discussing?

ANGEL #13: Gabriel is telling us about his time with Mary. *(Angel Organizer nods her head approvingly.)*

GABRIEL: Mary knew that her people were looking for a Messiah, but she had difficulty understanding how she could conceive the Son of God. I explained that the Holy Spirit would come upon her and the power of the Most High would overshadow her. I also told her of not-so-young Elizabeth's miracle baby, reminding her that nothing was impossible with God.

ANGEL #12: Mary didn't understand fully, but she said yes to God anyway.

ANGEL #4: Can you beat that! My charge needs me again! *(Leaves.)*

ANGEL #7: I remember Mary praising the Lord for the privilege of allowing her to be His servant.

25

ANGEL #6: Then she went and spent three months with Elizabeth, who was waiting for the birth of her baby. That was a special time for both women.

ANGEL #8: And bless Joseph's heart, it was tough to find that Mary was pregnant with a baby that was not his.

ANGEL #10: Gotta go in a hurry! *(Leaves.)*

(Angel #9 and Angel #5 return.)

ANGEL #18: But Joseph was in tune with God, and so God sent me down to tell him a dream about Mary's baby. Joseph without question took Mary home as his wife and has been caring for her.

(Angel #3 returns.)

ANGEL ORGANIZER: Come on! The day is getting away! We must practice even though some are gone. Jesus will be born tonight. We are supposed to announce this to the world.

(Everyone gets excited and they talk vigorously among themselves.)

ANGEL ORGANIZER: Hey! Let's settle down. We have to practice and the time is getting short. God reminded me this was the most important day the world has ever known, and everything has to be *absolutely perfect*, according to His plan. God wants us *all* to be there.

ANGEL #13: Now how can that be? You can see for yourself. We have to keep running back and forth to earth to take care of our charges. Some of us are gone all of the time, it seems.

ANGEL ORGANIZER: Perhaps that's why God chose very late at night for His Son's birth. Most people will be sleeping. Tonight they'll have to get along without us for a short while.

EVERYONE: *(Mumbling . . . then)* Oh, O.K.

ANGEL ORGANIZER: Now this is the way it will go. Shepherds near
Bethlehem will be out in the fields tonight watching their
sheep. The skies will be clear, and the wind calm. Most
shepherds will be asleep while the sheep graze peacefully.
Then Angel 19, with a brilliant light, will burst forth
through the skies to announce to the shepherds that Jesus
is born. Of course, this will frighten them at first, but they
will listen. Then the rest of us will burst through the
atmosphere, lighting up the heavens even more
spectacularly.

*(Angel Organizer begins passing out slips of paper to everyone
while still speaking. Everyone eagerly and excitedly reads the
message.)* This is what we'll say together in chorus.

(She rearranges a few angels in where they are standing.) Now
let's try it. Angel 19, you stand here and say your part.
Then the rest of us will join around you.

(Angel #10 returns.)

ANGEL ORGANIZER: Start Angel 19.

ANGEL#19: "Do not be afraid, I bring you good news of great joy that
will be for all the people. Today in the town of David a
Savior has been born to you; he is Christ the Lord. This
will be a sign to you: You will find a baby wrapped in
clothes and lying in a manger." *(Luke 2:10-12)*

(Angel #18 and #7 return during the speaking.)

THE Angel Group: *(Smiling, looking heavenward waving arms in praise.)*
"Glory to God in the highest, and on earth peace, good
will toward men." *(Luke 2:14 KJV)*

ANGEL ORGANIZER: Then we'll sing beautiful praises to God and
leave. Neither heaven nor earth will have ever seen
anything like it.

ANGEL #4: *(Returns from earth out of breath, but speaks)* HEY! I've just come from earth again. It's *so sad.* My how the world does need a Savior.

ANGEL #7: Yes, it's so pathetic to see the fighting, and the hardships people put on each other and themselves too.

ANGEL #18: They have all but forgotten God's law. They prefer their own way, instead of God's way. In self-centered living, they eventually self-destruct.

ANGEL #10: Many people frantically seek peace, something to satisfy. They look every way except for God's way.

ANGEL #16: God has gone to enormous ends to get people to see how much He loves them. But their sin blinds them. Jesus is God's only Son, and His birth into the world is the *only hope* the world has. But that's powerful Good News for all people who accept Him.

ANGEL #5: Oh, that all people everywhere will receive Christ into their hearts and lives.

GABRIEL: *(Turns to the audience and says:)* YES, BE SURE CHRIST IS YOUR PERSONAL SAVIOR, LORD AND KING THIS CHRISTMAS. Then you can rejoice with the angels by singing with us the first and last verses of *"Joy to the World."* *(or another song.)*

BIRTHDAY REFLECTION

PLACE—Home of Mary's Mother

TIME—Two years after Christ's birth. The family left Egypt and is just arriving in Nazareth.

CHARACTERS—*They should feel the message enough to add to the conversation spontaneously and appropriately to create realism. The four characters are:*

NARRATOR   MARY

JOSEPH   MARY'S MOTHER

Note: No two-year-old could be still, pretending to be asleep during this dialogue. Either use a life-sized doll or make a bundle of something about the appropriate size, covering it with a crude-looking blanket.)

SCENE—*Simple. Authenticity not required. A door to enter, a corner where the "boy Jesus" can be put to bed on the floor, and three chairs.*

COSTUMES: *Mary should have a big shawl, blanket or fabric yardage to cover her head and shoulders. Mother can wear a smaller, lighter-weight one around her shoulders. An old bathrobe will work for Joseph.*

(Mother is sitting at home alone, looking lonely.)

Narrator: Mary, Joseph, and the young Boy Jesus are just coming back to Nazareth from Egypt. It's late in the evening as they pull up to Mary's widowed mother's home. Jesus, so exhausted from the trip, doesn't stir as Joseph removes Him from His mother's arms. Mary knocks on the door of her mother's house.

(Knock at the door. Mother reluctantly gets up and heads for the door.)

MOTHER: Who is it?

MARY: It's us, Mother—Mary, Joseph, and our baby.

(Mother quickly opens the door, bursting with excitement as she hears and sees the family. She grabs Mary to give her a big hug. Then carefully she pats

Joseph on the shoulder as he holds the sleeping Child. She lifts the blanket and takes an admiring—grandmotherly peak.)

Narrator: *(Wait until all action takes place as described before speaking. Grandmother restrains her joy and relief momentarily, so the sleeping Boy is not disturbed. Mother then motions to them to bring the sleeping Boy over to the corner, where Joseph lays Him down. Her face beams radiantly as she clasps her hands together at bosom level and looks down at the sleeping child. A mixture of pride and awe should be portrayed by Mary's mother.)*

After Jesus is bedded down, Mary's mother stands to admire her Grandson briefly. They move away from the sleeping quarters to the sitting area. The couple, though very tired, is eager to share with Mary's mother something about the happenings of the past two years.

(Adults leave sleeping area and stand near stools or chairs.)

MOTHER: *(Still excited, she steps up and gives Mary another hug.)* PRAISE JEHOVAH! I am so happy! I can hardly believe you are really here. I wondered if I would ever see you again, my precious Mary, and you, *(steps over to give Joseph a hug)* dear Joseph, and my BEAUTIFUL Grandson. I'm so glad to see Him. Isn't he something? I can hardly wait to get acquainted with Him. *(A slight pause.)* Please, you're so tired; *(motions for them to be seated)* let's sit down. *(They sit down.)*

MARY: I began to wonder if I'd ever see you again too, Mother. It feels so good to be back home. And you're looking well.

JOSEPH: Yes, it's wonderful to see you again. We've been homesick to see you and others of our family and friends here in Nazareth. We're eager to get caught up on all the news.

MOTHER: Things surely didn't go the way we planned them, did they?

MARY: I'll say not. When our families began to plan our marriage, we thought a baby was a long way off. But God had other plans.

JOSEPH: And looking back, even though we don't understand it all yet, through all of the many strange happenings, we've been very aware of Jehovah's leadership and protection.

MOTHER: Mary, after you told your father about Gabriel's visit with you, he diligently searched the Scriptures. He studied every prophecy he could find concerning the coming of our Messiah. At first, I'll admit, we had mixed emotions. But as we understood more, we knew God had honored our family as no other had ever been. Even though your father was so ill, he was excited God was sending His Son to the world, and that you had been chosen to be His mother. He explained several things to me, including that the Messiah was to be born in Bethlehem.

MOTHER: Yes, at the time it seemed so unreasonable that Caesar should require Mary and me to go to Bethlehem. But God used him to fulfill that prophecy, even though old Caesar never knew it.

MARY: It was so difficult to leave you then, Mother, especially so soon after Father's death. How has it been?

MOTHER: I've been cared for very well. Your brothers and sisters understood how I missed your father, as well as you and Joseph. They knew about my concern over you . . . your hard trip with your due date so soon. They were a great comfort to me and have looked after me very well. But most of all, the Lord has been my Comforter. Many nights when I felt so alone and tempted to worry, He ministered to my spirit and gave me peace. Nothing helps a Mother more than to know her children are in God's will. He watches over His own in a special way. I know that more than I know anything.

MARY: How precious to hear you witness to that, dear Mother. *(Slight pause)* Perhaps Joseph and I should fill you in on some of the highlights, and then we all *must* get some rest.

MOTHER: Oh yes, I want to hear.

JOSEPH: Our traveling group arrived in Bethlehem on an evening a few days after we left here. We were all so weary, and of course, everyone was concerned for Mary. We all needed lodging, but the town was bursting with all kinds of travelers like us. I tried every place that kept lodgers, but there was just no room.

MARY: As we stopped at that last place, the innkeeper followed Joseph out to where I was sitting on the donkey. He saw my condition and pain, and quickly helped us find a place where we could bed down for the night.

JOSEPH: Yes, he found a cave nearby which was normally used as a sheep shelter. The shepherds and sheep were out for the night. And the place had recently been cleaned with fresh straw strewn around. The stable keeper kindly made a place for us, providing us with some privacy.

MOTHER: Do you mean my grandson was born in a stable?

MARY: Yes, Mother. But the occasion was so special. Joseph took wonderful care of me. I had no fear. God's presence filled that place. And when Jesus came, somehow I could hear all of heaven singing in my thoughts. And more astounding things happened later that night.

JOSEPH: We wrapped Baby Jesus in some cloths and blankets we had brought with us—that you helped to provide. A manger was there and made a perfect place for the Baby to sleep.

MARY: We had just gotten ourselves settled and were resting, when all at once we heard men's voices outside, coming toward the stable.

MOTHER: Was it the shepherds bringing their sheep back into the fold?

JOSEPH: It was shepherds all right, but they had left their sheep back in the fields. As the shepherd voices became more distinct, we could hear them praising God.

MARY: They came, wanting to see the Baby Jesus.

MOTHER: But how did they know?

MARY: Oh, that's the incredible party of the story.

JOSEPH: Right! Here's what the shepherds told us. Everything was quiet. The animals with their bellies full, and the men had just settled down for rest and sleep. Suddenly, the sky overhead lit up . . . with a . . . a fiery glow or brilliant light. They were so scared.

MARY: All at once, an angel appeared and told them not to be afraid. For that night in David's town of Bethlehem, a Savior was born. . . The Messiah. As proof, the shepherds could go there and find the baby lying in a manger.

JOSEPH: Then the sky filled with angels everywhere. They were praising God, saying, "Glory to God in the highest, and on earth peace and good will." *(Luke 2:14 KJV)*

MARY: After the angels disappeared, the shepherds lost no time in coming to see our precious little boy, God's only begotten Son.

JOSEPH: They came praising God, and they praised Him even more as they left. We were awed by it all.

MOTHER: Well, it seemed so sad that the Son of God had to be born in a stable, but no baby ever had a birth announcement like that one. It must have been something to experience.

MARY: When we took the baby to the temple in Jerusalem eight days later, we had more surprises.

MOTHER: Oh yes, that was the time for circumcision and for His name to become officially Jesus, as Gabriel had told you it must be.

JOSEPH: Yes, we carefully followed the Law and presented Jesus as

33

our firstborn to the Lord. Then we offered a proper sacrifice.

MARY: Simeon at the Temple recognized immediately that Baby Jesus was the Messiah. He told us about a revelation he had had . . . that he would see the Messiah before he died. That again made us realize that God was getting out the word about the birth of His Son—especially to those who were most sincerely looking for Him.

MOTHER: That is something! *(shakes her head in amazement)*

MARY: But that's not all. The very old prophetess, Anna, recognized Jesus as the Messiah too. When I stop and think about all of this, I'm nearly overwhelmed. I don't understand it all, and I never cease to be amazed.

MOTHER: You have been blessed above all other women, Mary. You have been directly involved in God's plan of salvation. Praise Jehovah!

MARY: I know, Mother, but some of it has been difficult too.

JOSEPH: Yes. We settled into a house soon after our trip to the Temple. We thought our life would take on some kind of normalcy then until Jesus got a bit older. I began doing a little carpentry work.

MARY: Things were going smoothly, until more visitors arrived.

MOTHER: Who were they?

JOSEPH: These were educated people who studied stars. They had traveled from the East following *one special star.* Even though they were not Jews, they were looking for the King of the Jews.

MARY: They stopped at King Herod's, thinking he could help them. So Herod asked the chief priests and teachers of the Law where the Christ was to be born.

JOSEPH: They told him Bethlehem. So he gave the Magi the information. Then he asked them to stop by on their way back. *(Using sarcasm in voice)* He said he wanted this information so he could come and worship Him too.

MARY: You can imagine our astonishment when we saw those dignified, richly-dressed men coming to see Jesus. When they saw Him, they immediately bowed down to worship Him. Then, they gave Him expensive gifts—gold, myrrh, frankincense. We could hardly believe their generosity.

JOSEPH: We were really surprised to hear that Herod was interested in Jesus too. But after they left, an angel of the Lord appeared to me and told me to take Mary and the Baby, and flee into Egypt. Herod wanted to know where Jesus was to kill Him, not worship him.

MARY: Those generous gifts helped to pay for food and shelter in Egypt.

JOSEPH: After Herod died, an angel appeared to me again, telling me to return to Israel. And here we are.

MOTHER: Never in my wildest imaginations. . . .*(shaking head in disbelief)*.

MARY: Oh, but Mother, this dear baby boy has been so good through it all. It's been truly amazing to see how responsive He's been as we've watched Him grow and develop. Sometimes He seems like a typical little boy, and sometimes I feel He knows more than I do. God's Son is no common child.

JOSEPH: Yes, even we worship Him as Messiah. He is Wonderful, Savior, Lord, Almighty God. He is King of Kings and Lord of lords! Oh, how our hearts rejoice.

MARY: *(looking upward)* "My soul glorifies the Lord and my spirit rejoices in God my Savior, for he has been mindful of the humble state of his servant. From now on all generations will call me blessed, for the Mighty One has done great things for me—holy is his hame. His mercy extends to those who fear him, from generation to generation." PRAISE HIS HOLY NAME! *(Luke 1:46-50)*

MOTHER: *(Gets to her feet quickly; lifts her eyes and her hands toward heaven; and progressively increases the intensity of each phrase as she speaks them.)* "PRAISE THE LORD, O MY SOUL; ALL MY INMOST BEING, PRAISE HIS HOLY NAME." *(Psalm 103:1) (Mary and Joseph stand and join her in praise.)*

ALL THREE: PRAISE JEHOVAH! PRAISE THE LORD MY GOD! PRAISE JEHOVAH.

CHRISTMAS BELLS AND BLESSINGS

CAST—

    *CHILDREN, all ages, as many or few as you want, plus these:
        MAUDE BYRNES—an elderly lady
        MRS. HAMILTON—Christmas program leader
        MRS. JOHNSON—nurse
    JERRY—ten-years-old or so, great-grandson of Maude Byrnes
        STEVE—Jerry's fun-loving friend
        KEITH—friend of Jerry's
    STACIE—repeats herself frequently, another friend
        KARA—another friend
        JILLIAN—another friend

*Speaking parts are included for 20 children, Child A *through* Child T. *These are in addition to the ones named above. Actually, this play can be done with as few as 10 children and 3 adults by giving* Children A through T *five parts each. If you give the characters named above all parts, you can do the play with less. Maude Byrnes could also become Claude Byrnes, if that works better. Adapt to your situation.*

EXPANSION IDEAS—*1) Include other songs. 2) Children could also take a small tree when they go to see Mrs. Byrnes, and then decorate it quickly while there. 3) Parts of the Christmas story could be acted out (in costume) while a narrator reads the parts for Child A through T. Make that part as elaborate as wanted. 4) Include a handbell song or medley.*

SETTING—*Place something like a hospital bed with a stand beside it at back-center stage, side-angled, foot forward. If a tree for Mrs. Byrnes is not decorated in the play, put a poinsettia or small decoration on the stand. Either a curtain or two portable folding dividers/screens should hide this scene. Allow enough room in front for the kids in the opening scene. For the second scene, merely remove screens and push the bed and stand forward.*

ITEMS NEEDED—*Bells, most any size or kind. Include some sleigh bells, if possible. Place a small pitcher with water and glass on the bedside stand.*

TO START: SING—*Children enter the sanctuary/auditorium single file, parading up and down the aisles while ringing bells (with or without accompaniment). Take as much or little time with this as wanted. Conclude the march by lining the children up front in readiness to sing this song (tune—"Jingle Bell" chorus):*

Christmas bells, Christmas bells,
Ring them loud and clear.
Christ was born in Bethlehem
To bring us love and cheer. . . .
Christmas bells, Christmas bells,
Ring so all can hear.
Jesus brought us second birth
And wipes away our tears.

(REPEAT one time. Then when the children move toward their predetermined place, have them place their bell in a box en route.)

Scene 1

TIME—After the Christmas program on Sunday.

SETTING—Front stage, in front of curtain or screens. **Steve, Jillian, Stacie,** *and* **Keith** *are standing and talking together.*

STEVE: We did it, guys! How bad were we?

JILLIAN: Oh, Steve, you're just fishing for a compliment. I think we all did okay. Everybody seemed to enjoy it.

KARA: Before it started, I was so scared. I even asked Mrs. Hamilton to pray for me. So when everything started, it was just like talking at home.

KEITH: Mrs. Hamilton must be glad the program is over. We gave her a rough time in practice, I think.

STACIE: But she's a neat lady and was patient with us, even though we didn't deserve it. Yes, even though we didn't deserve it.

STEVE: She didn't give up on us in practice, even when some parts sounded hopeless.

KEITH: I watched Mrs. Hamilton during the program, and I think she was very pleased with how things were going.

JILLIAN: Yeah, she even seemed proud of us.

STACIE: It was really fun. I'm sorry it's all over. Now we have to wait for three more days until Christmas . . . . *(shaking her head)* three more days . . . three more days until Christmas.

(Everyone groans in agreement.)

KEITH: What will we do now? School's out, nothing to do but wait. Three whole days. Yuck!

(Enter—Kara, bursting with news.)

KARA: Hey, you guys, do you know what I just heard?

STEVE: Of course! We hear everything you hear . . . just a bit delayed, that's all.

(Everyone laughs, nodding their heads in agreement with Steve.)

KARA: *(A bit perturbed, yet taking it good-naturedly.)* Oh, STEVE! This is serious!

STEVE: I'm sorry, but what have *we* heard that's new?

KEITH: Yeah, What's up, Kara? tell us.

(Others nod in agreement.)

KARA: Jerry's great-grandma fell and broke her hip yesterday.

JILLIAN: Oh, that's too bad. But she's rather old, isn't she?

STACIE: *(Nodding her head)* Yeah, she's really old—really, really, really old.

KARA: Did you notice Jerry looking so blue this morning?

STEVE: Well, now that you mention it, yes. He was somewhat quiet, not excited like the rest of us.

KEITH: He shouldn't feel too bad; she is old. And things like that sometimes happen to old people.

KARA: Even though Mrs. Byrnes is old, she still hurts as much as you and I do when we get hurt. And she is special to Jerry. He visits her a lot. He even stays overnight sometimes at her house.

STACIE: Yes, I know Jerry really liked her . . . yeah, really liked her.

(Enter—Jerry, unsmiling, looking gloomy)

JILLIAN: Say, Jerry, we just heard about Mrs. Byrnes, your great grandma. Tell us what happened.

JERRY: Well, it happened yesterday while we were practicing here. She fell as she stepped outdoors to get her newspaper. Somebody saw her and called the ambulance. After she got in the hospital, the doctors operate and put a pin in her hip.

STEVE: They pinned her up, eh? How do they do that?

(Others show amusement on their faces, but don't laugh.)

JERRY: Oh, Steve, it isn't funny. The doctors fixed it so it will heal right.

KEITH: Did she get along okay, Jerry?

JERRY: She went through the surgery fine. We stopped to see her this morning on the way to church. She was wide awake and talked with us okay.

STEVE: That should make you feel better.

JERRY: She'll do okay, but the sad thing is this. She had counted on coming to our Christmas program. She had helped me learn my lines and was really disappointed she couldn't see me in the program. But that's not the worst of it.

KARA: Oh? What's the worse part, Jerry?

40

JERRY: You all know that Grandma Byrnes is pretty old, don't you?

(Everyone nods in agreement and anticipates what more he has to say.)

JERRY: Well, she's 86 years old, and she's never missed a Christmas program in all of these 86 years, that is . . . *(sadly)* not until today.

STACIE: WOW-EEE! That's a lot of programs to see all right, a lot of programs—86, a lot of programs. My! My! My!

JERRY: Missing the program was giving her more pain than her hip. She was disappointed that she'd miss her first Christmas program ever.

JILLIAN: Hmmmmmm . . . Mr. Hamilton did make a video of it, didn't he?

KEITH: Yes, that's right, he did! My mom will want a copy of it, I know she will.

STEVE: Let's ask Mrs. Hamilton if Jerry's grandma can see the tape. Here she comes now.

(Enter Mrs. Hamilton)

JERRY: That would be almost like being here . . . but not quite.

MRS. HAMILTON: Why all the gloomy likes, kids? You did a fantastic job this morning. The Lord helped us, and we should all be happy and thankful.

KARA: But we just heard about Jerry's great-grandma Byrnes missing her first Christmas program *ever* in 86 years, because of a broken hip.

MRS. HAMILTON: Yes, I know. That's really a shame.

STACIE: We wondered if somebody could take the video over to the hospital for her to see . . . so she can see . . . so she can see all of it.

Mrs. Hamilton: We could do that okay, but I can think of a better idea that will require your help.

Keith: Oh, you can count on us Mrs. Hamilton. How can we help?

Mrs. Hamilton: I've been in the church office making a few telephone calls. Mrs. Johnson, the nurse at the hospital, talked with Mrs. Byrnes' doctor and the hospital administrator. I arranged for us to go to the hospital tomorrow, and present our program to her in her room.

Jerry: *(Breaking into a smile)* Do you really mean it?

Mrs. Hamilton: Yes, knowing Mrs. Byrnes, she's happiest when she's surrounded by her church family. The video will be nice, but us coming in person will be better.

(Everyone gets excited and chatters among themselves briefly.)

Jillian: That's a great idea. And we want to help. But what if everybody can't go?

Mrs. Hamilton: Almost everyone will go, I'm pretty sure. I've already talked to some of your parents. We may have to make a few adjustments—like maybe fewer bills. Mrs. Johnson said the other bed in the room is empty, so they would just push it out to make room for us.

Jerry: Wow! Taking our program to Grandma Byrnes. *(His face really lightens up as he thinks about it. Mrs. Hamilton smiles and nods her head.)* Oh, that's exciting; I can hardly wait. She'll be so happy. I know she will. And so will I.

Mrs. Hamilton: You had a hard time being happy this morning, Jerry, and I knew why. But I knew Mrs. Byrnes was even sadder. Well, kids, we can do it, if you'll come.

Everyone: *(Taking turns)* I will.

Mrs. Hamilton: But there's one catch.

KARA: What's that?

MRS. HAMILTON: A hospital is a place for sick and hurting people. We must be on our best behavior—quiet, except when it's time for doing our parts. No running around or goofing off. You must be on your very bet behavior. We don't want to make someone sicker by our being there.

STEVE: Oh, Mrs. Hamilton, we won't let you down. We'll be there and we'll be angels . . . perfect angels. *(Everyone bursts into laughter.)* I guess that's appropriate for Christmas, isn't it?

(Everyone nods as the laughter subsides.)

MRS. HAMILTON: I know I can trust you. I'll contact your parents about the time and transportation. We're going to make sure Mrs. Byrnes doesn't miss her 86th Christmas program, aren't we?

EVERYONE: Yeah! *(Everyone cheers and is happy.)*

STACIE: You know, this will help shorten our three-day wait for Christmas.

MRS. HAMILTON: And you'll be making good use of your waiting time. This will be a special gift given from each of you.

KARA: Yes, we talked about that in Sunday school class. If we give to someone who gives to us, that's not giving much.

KEITH: Our Sunday school teacher called that just a gift exchange, not really gift giving.

STEVE: Until now, I couldn't think of a way to really give of myself at Christmas without getting in return.

(Kids nod in agreement.)

MRS. HAMILTON: Hey! You kids are great. I'm impressed that you want to give of yourself to the Lord this Christmas. When we do it for people in need, such as Mrs. Byrnes, it's really doing it for Jesus. You've caught an important message of Christmas.

JERRY: Everyone will be giving a present of themselves to my grandma and to Jesus at the same time. That's the real spirit of Christmas, isn't it? I never thought of that before.

MRS. HAMILTON: That's right, Jerry. Listen, I have to go now. And I know your parents are waiting for you, so I'll see you all tomorrow. Bye.

EVERYONE: Bye! *(To Mrs. Hamilton and then to each other.)* *(Kids leave going in various directions.)*

Scene 2

TIME—The next day.

SCENE—In the hospital room. Mrs. Byrnes is in bed.

(Mrs. Johnson pours water into a glass for Mrs. Byrnes. She hands it to her, but Mrs. Byrnes has something to say first. . .)

MRS. BRYNES: You'd think an 98-year-old woman ought to be old enough to know how to take a disappointment, wouldn't you? But I wish I could have waited until after Christmas to break my hip . . . that is if I had to do it. I'm so disappointed. . . .

MRS. JOHNSON: We don't get to choose the time when bad things happen. But your disappointment is a good sign. It means you still love life and people, and like to be involved in church. That's good. And when it comes to Christmas, we never cease to be children—at least most of us. So don't be too hard on yourself.

(Mrs. Byrnes takes a few sips of water. Then Mrs. Johnson puts glass back on the stand.)

(A slight sound of bells from a distance is heard.)

MRS. BRYNES: Did you hear a bell, Mrs. Johnson? Or is that heaven beckoning to me? *(With a grin on face)*

MRS. JOHNSON: Now you may be the first patient I've ever had that had a problem with hearing bells.

(Both women laugh. Children should be ready to enter.)

(Children enter singing "Christmas Bells" with two children ringing either sleigh bells or little bells. They gather around her bed, wherever there is room, everyone facing toward Mrs. Byrnes and the audience.)

(Mrs. Byrnes is so surprised, but she claps her hands together in glee, smiling broadly. Jerry goes up close to her, gives her a hug, and sits by her on the bed.)

MRS. BRYNES: MY, OH MY, OH MY! What's all the commotion? I really did hear bells, didn't I?

JERRY: We've come so you won't have to miss the Christmas program this year.

MRS. BRYNES: *(Happy, but emotional, wiping tears)* What! You mean you've brought the Christmas program to me?

JERRY: That's right, Grandma. Mrs. Hamilton and the kids all wanted to come and do it for you.

MRS. BRYNES: This may be the best program ever—given just for my sake.

KARA: Oh, no, Mrs. Byrnes, not for you only. We really didn't have anything else to do, with school out and everything.

STACIE: That's right, and when we heard you hadn't missed a Christmas program in 86 years, well, we just had to . . . we just had to come and do it for you.

STEVE: Mrs. Byrnes, haven't you gotten tired of all those Christmas stories and programs after 85 years of them?

MRS. BRYNES: Oh no, no, no, never. Christmas is precious to me because it's a time to remember when my Savior came to earth.

KARA: But you can't remember all of them, can you?

MRS. BRYNES: No, but my parents told me about those very early ones many times. I was born on Thanksgiving Day. And we had a lot of snow that year. We lived about a mile from the church. It as too far to walk in such cold weather. And my daddy couldn't drive our Model T Ford car through the deep snow. So he hitched up our horse to the sleigh, and we rode it to church.

KEITH: Wow! Ride to church in a sleigh? What did they do with the horse during church? Wouldn't he run away?

MRS. BRYNES: *(laughing)* Oh, no. There was a hitching post out in front of the church that they tied the horse to. Our family wasn't the only one who came with a sleigh and horse. My father made it a family tradition for many years, for our family to go to the Christmas program at church on Sunday night in our sleigh . . . that is, if there was enough snow. When I heard the bells and heard your son, you really touched a chord of remembrance in my mind. Thanks kids for coming. It's so wonderful for you to come. *(Wiping a tear from her eye)*

(Kids listen to her with interest and almost envy.)

MRS. HAMILTON: Well, kids, we'd better get started with our program. We can't stay too long or we will tire Mrs. Byrnes.

MRS. BRYNES: I don't think you'll do that, Mrs. Hamilton. These youngsters coming with their program is powerful medicine for me.

*(Throughout the program, **Mrs. Byrnes** should show much enjoyment. She should respond to each child with a smile and nod.)*

(Mrs. Hamilton signals to the kids to that it's time to start singing "Christmas Bells" and they sing it through twice.)

(Jerry stands ready to speak.)

JERRY: When I hear the bells on Christmas day,
As they, the familiar carols play,
I think of that old story so sweet.
Christ came to make salvation complete.

CHILD A: Yes, Jesus came from heaven to earth that day.

CHILD B: This is what happened.

CHILD C: The angel Gabriel came to visit Mary, and told her that she had found favor in God's sight. She would become the mother of the Messiah—who was Jesus.

CHILD D: Now Mary was pledged to marry Joseph. So an angel of the Lord appeared to him in a dream.

CHILD E: The angel told Joseph to go ahead with plans to take Mary as his wife. Her Baby was from the Holy Spirit, the very SON OF GOD.

CHILD F: Then the angel told him that when the Baby would be born, He must be named Jesus, because He would save His people from their sins.

CHILD G: When the time came near for Jesus to be born, Joseph and Mary were required by the Roman government to go to Bethlehem.

CHILD H: There was no room for them to stay in that town, except in a stable. So Jesus was born there, wrapped in cloths and slept in a manger.

CHILDREN: *(Sing)* "Away In a Manger"

CHILD I: Shepherds were watching their sheep that night out in the fields.

CHILD J: And behold, an angel of the Lord came through the skies. The glory of the Lord was brilliantly shining.

Child K: The angel told him, "Do not be afraid. I bring you good news of great joy that will be for all the people." *(Luke 2:10)*

Child L: "Today in the town of David a Savior has been born to you; he is Christ the Lord." *(Luke 2:11)*

Child M: "This will be a sign to you: You will find a baby wrapped in strips of cloth and lying in a manger." *(Luke 2:12)*

Child N: Then many, many angels appeared with him, "praising God and saying, `Glory to God in the highest, and on earth peace to men on whom his favor rests.' "

Child O: Then the shepherds went to Bethlehem to see the Baby Jesus.

Child P: They bowed down and worshiped him. But they weren't the only visitors Jesus had.

Child Q: Then the shepherds went into Bethlehem to see the Baby Jesus. A star had led them to Bethlehem. They brought Jesus gifts of gold, myrrh, and incense.

Child R: Jesus' coming to earth was the best news ever, and still is. Christmas bells ringing remind us of that good news.

Child S: When we accept Jesus as our Savior, then we can keep those bells ringing.

Child T: Yes, we are to let the whole world know that Jesus was born. And that He came to forgive us of our sins, and to give us new life.

Children: *(sing)* "Ring the Bells"

Mrs. Brynes: *(Using every expression of joy possible)* Oh, this is the best Christmas program ever. You all did so well. And now I can still say, I've never missed a program.

Jerry: Grandma, next year you can go to church to see the Christmas program.

MRS. BRYNES: I hope so. But when you get to be my age, one never knows. One thing I do know is that if I'm at all able, I'll be there. But one of these Christmases, I won't be here to go. When that happens, don't be sad. There's only one thing better than celebrating Christmas here on earth.

JERRY: *(Frowns and has a puzzled look)* And what could that be?

MRS. BRYNES: Celebrating Christmas in heaven with Jesus. Oh, that will be even more grand and glorious than what the shepherds saw that night when Jesus was born. Yes, kids, I've spent most of these 86 years preparing for that time when I meet Him face-to-face. I will join those who have gone before. And we'll have eternity to celebrate with Jesus.

JERRY: *(Still looking a little sad)* But I'll miss you then, Grandma.

MRS. BRYNES: Oh, precious Jerry, *(She pats him on the shoulder.)* I'll miss you too, but you know what? I'm going to be watching and waiting for you up there. Someday you can come and we'll celebrate together . . . forever and ever. In fact, I'm going to be watching and waiting for all of you up there. I'll be ready to welcome you when you come. *Now don't forget!*

JERRY: I'll remember, Grandma. I'll always remember.

THE Others: *(Everyone nods in agreement)* Yes, we'll all remember.

STEVE: The bells will really be ringing in heaven, won't they?

MRS. BRYNES: Oh yes, and they will be more beautiful than any we've ever heard.

(The kids get excited a bit when she says this.)

MRS. BRYNES: Your Christmas program here today was the best one ever for me. You came, giving of yourself to me with this program. That's the best gift anyone can receive or give.

KARA: Oh yes! But we were wrong when we said we could give to you today, without getting anything back. I think we actually received more than we gave.

CHILDREN: *(Quickly and heartily agree)* Yes! Yes!

MRS. BRYNES: That's nice. The Bible says, "It's more blessed to give than to receive." *(Acts 20:35 KJV)*. Say, I know it's getting time for you to go, but I have one more favor to seek of you. Will you sing "Joy to the World" for me?

MRS. HAMILTON: Sure, we'll sing it. And I'm going to ask everyone else to stand and sing it with us. *(Motions for everyone to stand.)*

SONG—*"Joy to the World" (EVERYONE SINGS)*

PORTRAITS OF MARY

by Hazel Jaycox Brown

PLACE AND TIME—Here. *Mary publicly shares with an audience a series of present tense portraits coming from different times in her life.*

CHARACTERS—*One or more narrators will fill in the gaps. Mary is the focus, but two or three different women could portray her as she ages. Her part should be well in mind, but she may keep a script in front of her for reference, if needed.*

SCENE—*The narrator and Mary can speak from the same lectern. A spotlight or candles focused on Mary while she speaks in a darkened room adds drama.*

COSTUME—*Mary should wear a plain, medium-to-dark colored dress. A change in her shawl and other little things are suggested as the script unfolds.*

NARRATOR: Mary, Mother of Jesus, will be portrayed here tonight *(today)* by _____. She, as Mary, will share a mother's perspective and probable emotions as she witnessed certain events in the life of Christ. Though the Scriptures provide us little about Mary, several things are implied. We know she was human, not divine. She failed to understand everything as it happened. The writer here has sought to stay within the Scriptures while prayerfully attempting to portray something of what it was like to be the mother of Jesus.

MARY: *(Shawl worn around the shoulder.)* I, Mary, am a young Jewish girl. It's the custom in our day for us to marry young—around age 14. So I am getting ready for such an occasion. Most marriages in our land are prearranged by the couple's families without consulting them. But in our area, Galilee, families often consider the wishes of their children.

I first noticed Joseph a few years ago. His father, a carpenter, has made several things for our family

51

through the years. Joseph has also learned the trade and does excellent work. I've gone with my father several times to his family's workshop. Joseph will provide a good living for me and our family.

I noticed how handsome Joseph was when I first saw him. We exchanged a few words then. I sensed he might be interested in me too. Every time my father and I went, Joseph and I managed a few moments to talk. Joseph loved Jehovah and freely praised Him. Yes, the more I saw of that man, the more I dreamed of becoming his wife.

You can imagine my excitement when Joseph's family approached mine about our possible marriage. My father wasn't surprised. He knew I was interested in Joseph. I believe we will be the happiest couple ever. Joseph IS special. He isn't rich, but we share a common desire to love and serve God. He and his family go to the synagogue weekly, just like mine. God will bless our marriage.

NARRATOR: Mary and Joseph had a firm foundation for which to start life together. But when Joseph's family approached Mary's, no one could have guessed what God's plan for that couple was. Jehovah was setting the stage, getting ready to send the promised Messiah to earth. Listen to Mary as she tells about Gabriel's appearance to her.

MARY: *(Different shawl and pulled over her head.)* It was early evening. I was alone by that big rock near our home. My thoughts were a mixture of praying to God and dreaming of life with Joseph. Suddenly, out of nowhere, a man stood in front of me. I jumped, then shuddered at his appearance. My first thought was to start walking . . . walking fast to get away from him. After a few steps, I could tell he had something to say to me. So I paused, and he said, "Greetings, you who are highly favored! The Lord is with you." I was scared. What was happening?

Then he told me his name was Gabriel. He said he

understood my fears, and tried to reassure me again by saying, "Do not be afraid, Mary, you have found favor with God." *(Luke 1:28, 30)*

It helped to hear him say that, for I wanted God's approval. I believed my approaching marriage to Joseph was His will. The Lord would surely bless our future together. But never in my wildest dreams did I think God could use me for anything significant.

And I wondered, could an angel really be talking with me, a woman, now? I believed they usually appeared to men, but even then on rare occasions.

Gabriel went ahead and explained that God had chosen me to be the mother of His only Son whom He was getting ready to send to earth. His name would be Jesus. He will be great and will be called the Son of the Most High. The Lord God will give him the throne of His father David, and he will reign over the house of Jacob forever; His kingdom will never end." *(Luke 1:32, 33)*

I was stunned. This was hard for me to grasp in my mind. Was I really going to give birth to the promised Messiah we Jews had been so long awaiting? Then it hit! I would be unmarried, and pregnant. But how could pregnancy occur when no man had never touched me? I stepped back away from Gabriel, wondering what would happen next.

He sensed my fear and quickly explained, "The Holy Spirit will come upon you, and the power of the Most High will overshadow you. So the holy one to be born will be called the Son of God." *(Luke 1:35)*

Then Gabriel told me about Elizabeth, my relative, who had been childless until now in her old age. And now she was in her sixth month. That was a miracle, I knew. Gabriel reminded me, ". . . Nothing is impossible with God." *(Luke 1:37)*

I believed that. But she was married, and everyone rejoiced with her. I would be a disgrace unless God intervened. Other questions I left unasked, but I wondered: Would my beloved Joseph believe my story? Even if he does, he might not want me for his wife. I knew how people talk and were so quick to condemn. If I publicly told the truth, everyone would laugh at me and accuse me of trying to cover my sin.

Then I began thinking about what an honor was being bestowed upon me—chosen by God for this most special task. With that thought, peace came to my heart, and I could inwardly pray: Yes, Lord, here am I. Accomplish Your will in my life. Joseph, my future, my family and friends are all in Your hands, Lord. And so is my reputation. I willingly accept Your plan.

I said to Gabriel, "I am the Lord's servant. . . . May it be to me as you have said."

NARRATOR: Let's ask ourselves these questions now: Am I now available to God for whatever He asks? Am I sometimes more concerned about being appropriate than being obedient? Am I willing to risk public and private ridicule for the cause of Christ? Am I willing to follow His will completely, even when I fail to understand? Will I do it without question, reservation or complaint?

Christmas is a good time to say, "Yes, Lord, I surrender to You. I submit my life to You right now. I will be your servant." *(Pause.)*

Now hear Mary's account of her visit with Elizabeth.

MARY: *(Another shawl, dress too maybe.)* Gabriel's mention of Elizabeth seemed to be a directive to me. So I went to visit her.

Upon arrival, I was uncertain about what to expect. Maybe Elizabeth wouldn't believe my story. But when greeting her, she exclaimed, "Blessed are you among women, and blessed is the child you will bear! But why am I so favored, that the mother of my Lord should come to me? As soon as the sound of your greeting reached my ears, the baby in my womb leaped for joy. Blessed is she who has believed that what the Lord has said to her will be accomplished." *(Luke 1:42-45)*

Elizabeth, filled with the Holy Spirit, knew of my condition before I could tell her. Even her unborn babe recognized the presence of God's Son.

This was a gift to me from the Lord. Jehovah was taking care of those in my family. Elizabeth would confirm my story. I rejoiced: I sang; my heart bubbled with praise. God is worthy of all my trust. The time with Elizabeth those next three months was precious. I helped with the housework, and she ministered to me. Near the time of her delivery I left. Others would care for her. I must face Joseph.

The Lord had been so very wonderful to me those first months. I kept telling myself not to worry, yet Joseph had every right to renege on his promise. Soon my secret would become visible, so a decision must be made. I worked to overcome my fears and to trust God fully.

NARRATOR: It requires an act of my will often, to trust God when circumstances are beyond my control. I, like Mary, must refuse to give in to doubts and fears. Now we'll hear about the outcome.

MARY: *(Wearing an earlier shawl around her shoulder):* Again, God was faithful. Of corse, Joseph was shocked to learn I was pregnant; that was natural. He wanted to believe my story, but it wasn't easy. He had the right to divorce himself from our commitment of marriage.

But Joseph was a righteous man, *and* he loved me. He didn't want me to live in public disgrace. He wrestled within himself. He prayed about it. Then he submitted to God's will. With this, an angel told him in a dream, "Joseph son of David, do not be afraid to take Mary home as your wife, because what is conceived in her is from the Holy Spirit. She will give birth to a son and you are to give him the name of Jesus because he will save his people from their sins." *(Matthew 1:20, 21)* He was then reminded of the prophecy in Isaiah, "The virgin will be with child and will give birth to a son, and they will call him, 'Immanuel'—which means, 'God with us.' " *(Matthew 1:23)*

Joseph never doubted after that. He took me home to be his wife and provided tender, loving care. Joseph never complained. He even joyfully anticipated the birth. And he never exercised his rights as a husband until after Jesus was born.

NARRATOR: We could take other events like this throughout Mary's life. But would take much time. However, have you ever asked yourself these question? How would Mary and Joseph feel about the mandate from Caesar Augustus that sent them to Bethlehem so near the baby's due date? Bethlehem was a difficult-to-travel 90 miles from Nazareth. But that was no excuse. A donkey helped, but the trip was treacherous. I wonder; had they realized Jesus was to be born in Bethlehem? If so, why did they wait until the last minute to travel?

Upon arriving in Bethlehem, a very weary Mary was either in labor or close to it. They couldn't find a place to stay. Joseph finally found a not-so-clean, empty stable. A corner would provide shelter and privacy. Mary must have wondered why God's Son had to be born in such miserable surroundings. Listen as she tells about their first visitors.

MARY: The stable wasn't as bad as it sounds. Joseph fixed a soft bed of straw for me in a corner. He placed bedding over it that we had brought with us. He worked hard to make things as easy as possible for me. God was with us in a very special way during delivery and afterward. We had such peace and joy.

But we were startled later in the night when we heard men's voices. As they neared we could hear them praising God. Those strangers were shepherds who had come straight from their flocks in the field. They knew about Jesus' birth. We asked how. And they described a supernatural scene—hard to believe. That birth announcement was awesome; the greatest any baby ever had.

NARRATOR: But more amazing things happened. Eight days later, Mary and Joseph took the Infant Jesus to the temple. This was the time for circumcision and for the offering a sacrifice as required by the Law.

MARY: It had never occurred to us that such extraordinary things might happen at the temple. When Simeon say Baby Jesus, he immediately recognized the Infant as the Son of God. He saw our amazement, and explained that the Holy Spirit had revealed to him that he would not die before he had seen the Lord's Christ. Then Simeon took Baby Jesus in his arms and praised God. He then blessed us as a family, but his last comment was unclear, "This child is destined to cause the falling and rising of many in Israel, and to be a sign that will be spoken against, so that the thoughts of many hearts will be revealed. And a sword will pierce your own soul too." *(Luke 2:34, 35)*

As we walked away from Simeon, Anna, an elderly widow who never leaves the temple, saw us. We had known of this saint of the Lord who worshiped day and night there, fasting and praying. But we were amazed when she immediately recognized that Baby Jesus was the Messiah. After giving thanks to God, she joyfully began witnessing to others.

NARRATOR: We know little about Jesus' infancy. They moved to a

57

house there in Bethlehem soon after Jesus' birth. Probably Joseph took on some carpentry jobs to provide for his family's needs.

Sometime before Jesus was two years old, they had more visitors. These were the Magi from the East. They came looking for the King of the Jews. These educated Gentiles, no doubt, had some knowledge of God and prophecy concerning the coming Messiah. They had revealed a long distance with only a start to direct them to Jerusalem. There they asked King Herod where this Baby was. His chief priests found in the Scriptures that Bethlehem was the place for the Baby to be born. So after telling the Magi, Herod asked them to return and tell him precisely where the Baby was. He wanted to go and worship Him too. But that was a lie.

As they left Jerusalem, the Magi were happy to see the star leading them again. It stopped at the house where the family lived in Bethlehem.

MARY: We had noticed that extraordinary star shining over our house, but we were unaware that it was bringing us company. When Joseph answered the door, we were astounded to see such sophisticated-looking visitors interested in our Baby. Their response upon seeing Him was something too. Immediately, they fell on their knees and began worshiping Him. Before leaving, the Magi gave Jesus very expensive gifts—gold, myrrh and frankincense.

NARRATOR: The Magi were warned in a dream not to return to Herod. After they left, an angel appeared to Joseph also in a dream and told him to take the family and flee to Egypt. Herod would search for the Child to kill Him.

Joseph and Mary didn't waste time. They left quickly that night, very much aware that God was looking after His own Son.

But, in time, it was safe enough to return to Nazareth.

Jesus had to learn to walk, talk, and had to be potty trained like any other child. Yet He was an amazing child, and the fact that the grace of God was upon Him was evident to Joseph and Mary.

Even though they had gone through all of this with Him, they were surprised with Jesus at age 12.

MARY: Jesus had always obeyed us. He knew that morning at the temple we were leaving for home with other families from Nazareth. We assumed that He was with us, walking with others His age. By evening we discovered He was missing. So we went back to look for Him. You can imagine how upset Joseph and I were when we couldn't find Jesus.

Three days later we finally found Him in the temple courts. He was sitting among the teachers there—listening and talking. We watched long enough to see what was happening. He was creating quite a stir by the way He fielded questions teachers were throwing at Him. Jesus knew things they didn't. His wisdom from God amazed them all.

When we went up to Him and told Him about our concern, He was surprised. "Why were you searching for me?" he asked. "Didn't you know I had to be in my Father's house?" *(Luke 2:49)*
Nevertheless, He returned with us. He recognized our authority over Him and grew up to be a fine young Man.

NARRATOR: Tradition says Joseph died while Jesus was still living at home in early manhood. Mary was left with younger children to care for. By law the eldest took over responsibility for the family when the father died. Mary, no doubt, leaned hard on Him. Jesus reliably handled that task until He left home at age 30. He knew what it was to raise children, to teach younger boys carpentry, to discipline them, to provide for them and to be a spiritual leader for the family. No doubt, Mary grew in her appreciation of Him during this time, as well as in her devotion to Him as Lord. The younger ones may have resented Him. None became followers until after His resurrection. Then they served Him wholeheartedly.

When Jesus left home, probably the rest of the family was grown enough to carry on the family business. Mary, with other women, cared for Jesus' and His disciples' personal needs. So she witnessed at least some of His preaching, teaching and miracles performed. She was proud of her Son.

Jesus had been good at solving problems at home. It was natural that Mary sought His help at the wedding of Cana. She knew the hosts were running out of wine. She knew Jesus could help, and sought Him. He seemed reluctant. But she unhesitatingly told the servants, "Do whatever He tells you." She never doubted His ability and His caring for those in need.

Being the mother of Jesus had its share of wonderful moments. But some things were difficult for her to understand. Yet her confidence and faith in Him was firm during those last events before Jesus' crucifixion.

MARY: (*Older*) I tried to see everything that week before Jesus' death. I suffered many emotional extremes those days! One day the crowd was ready to make Him king. Then a few days later, He was on trial with the crowd screaming, "Crucify Him! Crucify Him!"

I'd rejoiced with Mary and Martha when Lazarus was raised from the dead. But it then when tensions really began to build. As I helped to serve Passover in the Upper Room, I heard some of the conversation and what Jesus told His disciples. Then the next thing I knew, He'd been arrested. Everywhere I went I heard Jesus' enemies stirring up the people against Him. I couldn't hear and see everything, but to see Him stripped of His clothes, beaten and scourged unmercilessly—that was *hard* for me to bear. I wept. I cringed. I wondered why God seemed not to be taking care of His Son now. This horrendous cruelty continued even after He appeared to be nothing but a bloody mess of raw flesh. It was then I looked up and pleaded with God, *(Say this sentence slowly with great feeling)* "Please stop this madness, God. I can't bear it any more. REMEMBER, JESUS IS *MY SON* TOO!" *(Pause to gather your composure.)*

My emotions were raw. When they started nailing Him to that cross, I sobbed uncontrollably and pleaded for God's intervention again. His pain was my pain; I felt all of it and felt neither of us could bear any more. My head was pounding; my stomach wrenched. There was no comfort.

When Jesus cried, "My God, my God why have you forsaken me?" I realized God too, was suffering. But why would He forsake His Son? *I hadn't.* People were cruel; Jesus had done no wrong. I felt faint; my legs would hardly hold me. But John, aware of my condition, held onto me. To see Jesus crucified was hideous, I wanted to run. *But I couldn't leave Him to die alone.*

Jesus saw me during His suffering and was so concerned for me. He asked John to take responsibility for me. I strongly felt His precious love, but my heart was breaking.

NARRATOR: After his death she wanted His body to be taken care of properly, but she had no money for a tomb. Joseph of Arimathea offered an unused one he had. So he and Nicodemus removed the body from the cross and placed it in the tomb. Several women shared Mary's grief and helped to prepare spices and perfumes, as was the custom of that day.

MARY: I should have known this wasn't the end. Can you imagine how I felt when I found that Jesus was alive three days later? That first meeting was special, beyond

61

description. Yet our relationship was different. I saw Him primarily as my Savior and less as my Son. I battled over this while Jesus was in the grave. But His resurrection settled it all. Praise His Holy Name!

NARRATOR: How much time Mary spent with Jesus during His forty days on earth, we don't know. But during that time Mary understood His Father's business was foremost. I believe she saw Him ascend into Heaven. By then her faith was so strong, she anticipated something even better.

She gathered with the others in the Upper Room, prayed with them and received the Holy Spirit on the day of Pentecost. The Spirit of her Son and Savior, fully alive, now dwelt constantly within her in a brand new and better way. There would be no more separation. And she received new power to witness and work for God. She joyfully accepted it all and shared her story through Luke and his gospel.

Mary was important to God and His plan. She served Him faithfully, even through great human struggle. The victory was won in her life through her Son, just like it can be in you and me. She now lives in heaven joyously with her Son and Savior, God's Son, for ever and ever and ever.

This gift of God is available to you this Christmas? Won't you accept Him now?

Notes